Three Times Three

Also by Robert Flanagan

Books:

> *Maggot*, a novel, 1971
> *The Full Round*, poems, 1973

Chapbooks:

> *Not for Dietrich Bonhoeffer*, poems, 1969
> *Body Home*, poems, 1971
> *At the Edge of the Ghost Town*, poems, 1972
> *News from a Backward State*, poems, 1973
> *On My Own Two Feet*, poems, 1973
> *Three Times Three*, stories, 1977

THREE TIMES THREE

ROBERT FLANAGAN

Ithaca House
Court Street Chapbooks · 1977

Acknowledgment is made to the following magazines:
Bird Effort and *Fiction*.

Special thanks to Stan Sommer for his generous grant.

Cover photo by William Stafford.

Court Street Chapbook Series is edited, designed and
printed by Scott Sommer and Cecil Giscombe at Ithaca
House, 108 North Plain Street, Ithaca New York 14850.

To the memory of
Minnie Jane Treloar
& Robert John Flanagan

Contents

The Bear's Wife's Husband's Tale

"Take me as I am," she says.

I have many times, and enjoyed it. I am tempted to try it now. I want to believe we could gloss over in our mixed sweat the differences like cage bars between us.

She is kneeling before me, facing away: nakedness gives her the appearance of vulnerability. Her bowed head lets her long black hair fall forward to hide her face like a mourning veil. Her small shoulders give way to a widening, fat-rippled back and overflowing hips and buttocks. She is a promise of softness.

"Take me as I am."

But in the hand mirror she is holding I can see her eyes like bullet holes in the glass. I can tell she doesn't mean it that way this time. It's the other way, the bars between us. She thinks I am trying to change her.

"Hold still."

"Did I hide in the dark until we were married?"

"We've been all through that."

"Were you blind?"

"Hold still. If you move, I'll cut you."

"I know how you mean it. I know what you'd like to do."

"More than I do, I suppose."

"Yes."

There is no getting around her when she is like this. I take up the razor and bring it down across the broad flat plane of her shoulder. It leaves a path of creamless, hairless greyish-blue skin so clean I lean forward to kiss it. Her back shudders as if I had touched a high-strung horse.

"You're sick," she says.

"I am a normal man, a normal husband. I love you." I wipe flecks of shaving cream from the fringes of my mustache which was her insistent idea. We all make compromises. Why won't she see that?

I drag the razor against her skin, rinse it, do it again. The left shoulder is nearly cleared, making the right one, like her lower back and hips, clouded by curling dark hair, look all the worse.

"You're making me sick."

"Don't be melodramatic."

"I mean it," she says. "My stomach's turning."

"A bargain's a bargain."

"Don't remind me."

"I will. I am. You wanted to go camping, didn't you? Answer me."

She says something, her voice a hiss, which sounds like 'slave'. That theme again! "You're not a slave," I tell her, "You are a free adult. You want to go back on your word?"

"I said, 'shave'."

I do. My mind glitters with her clean-shaven image, the way she would let me make her when we were first married. Before her stiffening of intent. Why has she become so suspicious? Would she accuse a surgeon relieving her of a tumor of projecting an ideal upon her at the cost of her identity? "Hold still."

Afterwards, she wraps herself in a beige orlon-pile robe — I will not allow her to own furs — and sulks in the living room. The fire she has built in the grate cannot ease the shadow of her frown. The log flares and pops in the gloom of the house as if it were a handful of twigs burning in deep night woods.

"It's beautiful out here," she said.

It was cold and dark, empty of human company. I had agreed to go only because I could no longer stand her complaints. I had thought it would satisfy her and give me peace, but I knew as soon as I saw the look in her eyes the mistake I had made. Whenever we went berry-picking or camping she became animated and I would think it was to spark a change, but back home she again became distracted, morose, spent entire evenings pacing the living room or staring out a window.

The time before this, I had told her I could no longer bear it and her abrupt laughter shocked me it was so savage. I decided then that there would be no more picnics or camping. She would have to learn to live in the real world.

But she stopped shaving. I took it as long as I could. Nights, I would wake in our bed in the dark and hear breathing and reach for her. That she slept naked had struck me in the first weeks of our marriage as romantic. How quickly reflection overturns first impressions. To touch fur in the dark, my heart jerking like a snared rabbit!

Finally, a rational compromise was reached. We would vacation that fall in the mountains: She would resume shaving.

The trouble with reason is that it is one-dimensional; like an aerial photograph it hides the depths of caves which show up as flat black spaces, easily crossed. Experience teaches a man reason's limits, though by that time the fall may have broken both his legs.

"I don't think so."

"Hm?"

"That it's beautiful," I said "It's isolated."

"Is that how you feel?"

"You know how I feel."

"I know what you think."

"Don't start. That Noble Savage fantasy ended for me the same year my acne cleared up." I pushed out of my camp chair and lay another split log on the stone-circled fire. "Why don't you grow up?"

At the edge of the light she sat on a log, arms

4

wrapped about her knees, pressing them to her chest. She stared out at the surrounding woods, her eyes twin fires. I followed her look. A blank black wall rose up around us like a tidal wave.

I told her I loved her. I did. I was frightened of her too, but would not tell her. I barely allowed myself to guess it.

In the tent in our double bag she wanted me in her. She squirmed beneath me, grunting as if in pain. Later, she looped an arm under my head and held me to her breast, her free hand stroking my hair or lightly touching my mustache.

Who was trying to change whom?

"I'm having a drink. Do you want one?"

She pulls her robe more tightly about her, as if my words were a draft in the room. "You didn't adopt me."

"Do you want one?" I teeter on the brink of the room. I want a domestic scene; brandy in stemmed glasses, Tchaikovsky on the stereo, a discussion of recent political developments in Washington, her head on my arm, fine blond hair fanning out . . .

"No one made you my guardian."

But she refuses to cooperate in the slightest way. She wants to draw me into an argument, to go over and over the same old matters as if she were licking a wound.

"Or keeper."

"Why do you want to say things like that? To deliberately hurt me? Why can't you . . ."

"Show some gratitude?"

"I never said that." I turn back to face her.

"Because you're so charitable." She aims her words like an expert knife-thrower, bracketing the shape she has chosen for me.

"It has nothing to do with charity."

"Oh yes. To take in the poor girl who . . ."

"I didn't take you in. I married you."

"A poor widow."

"Goddamn it! You are not a widow!" She's won. Here we go.

At first the story was only another folk tale to me. A bear took a girl from the village. The men searched for her with no success, and the family performed the mourning rites. Three years later, the girl came to the family's hogan. She was black with dirt and fur. The mother was afraid at first, but the girl cried that she was her daughter. The mother took her in and scrubbed off the dirt and scraped some of the fur from her face and arms. That night the bear prowled the edge of the village, bawling. Some men killed him. The girl stayed on with her family, shunned by the others.

I had gone to the village to research primitive myths. But she was real. I watched, fascinated, as she moved about the hogan, silent and dark. The father would shake his head and look at his feet.

I encouraged the mother to regularly scrub and shave her daughter. I began helping the girl to remember the English she had learned before being carried off. We sat together for hours over school books, her eyes bright with intelligence, her voice softened by the pain of her experience.

During my stay, I took notes for a paper on the factual basis of animal-mate folktale. But when I left, she left with me, and I threw away my notes.

When we first started to talk to each other and she asked me if I hunted, I nearly lied. I wanted her respect and I knew the men of her village were hunters. But I told the truth: I had never seen any reason to hunt.

Even as I spoke, I was thinking of how to make her see my behavior in the proper context. The world I lived in was different than hers. Was it my courage she questioned? It took more courage to tell the truth, I thought, than to kill an animal. I was even prepared to tell her I was a vegetarian.

But my confession did not offend her. As I was about to speak further, she touched me for the first time. Despite its stubble, her hand on my wrist seemed to possess a feminine tenderness.

Now that I know her I realize the question that lay behind the question. But with both legs broken, the only way I can leave her is to crawl.

I would rather fight it out on my own ground. I can and will be firm. "Do you hear me? You are not a widow."

She stares at the log smoldering in the grate.

"Answer me!"

She nods her head. "I know."

"We have to live in the real world." She is silent. It seems settled. Perhaps this time for good. There will be no more wilderness camping. If we want a vacation, we can rent a cottage at the Cape. Or drive down to New Orleans. "I'll get you a drink."

I awake in the dark and think I am in a tent. The glow of the electric blanket switch anchors me. Her side of the bed is empty.

I surprised her the last night of the trip. I am stronger than I look. When I missed her, got out of the sleeping bag and discovered her at the edge of the clearing, I carried her back to camp. Perhaps she only half-struggled. It comforts me to think so. Still, I felt strong enough to bring her back no matter what she did.

The lights are out in the kitchen. She is looking out the window. I come up behind her. She is eating blueberries with her fingers from a pint box.

The Apprentice

I WANT TO TELL THE TRUTH ABOUT

the limits of stories. The apprentice at this form of magic asks "Will it work?", not "Is it true?". Shadows have more aesthetic possibilities than direct sunlight. Let Plato climb: I rummage about in the basement of the past.

DR. FRANKENSTEIN

is the hero I emulate. I am raising the dead to life. A boy, ten years old, twenty two years ago, sleeps in his bed. I exert my Psychic Power! and he slowly rises. He thinks to go to breakfast and then to school, but I suddenly speed up time and he is (charmingly unsuspecting of his actions being manipulated from the future) going to the living room after supper to curl up in an armchair with a comic book.

The story he is reading is about a scholar who discovers an old manuscript in a curio shop. The manuscript contains a cryptic formula which, when said aloud, gives one supernatural power: Spoken wishes come true. Naturally the scholar, the aging victim of an emotionally repressed life, misuses his gift to ask for "total power". Everything now depends upon his constant attention. The world begins falling apart around him. Furious (though the comic book doesn't state it, it is easy for us to see that the scholar's frustration is due to his basic wish — the creation of an ordered and satisfying life — lying beyond the power of words) he impulsively wishes he were dead.

But the boy stops at the curio shop scene, trying to read the writing in the manuscript in the comic book. He thinks that if he could only make it out, and say it . . .

In a three room apartment above an ammonia-smelling bar and grill, the only reading material besides his comic books being newspapers, a paperback of Dale Carnegie's *How to Win Friends and Influence People,* and his father's frayed, cloth-bound copy of his father's *Old Favourites,* a book of poems reprinted from the Family Herald, from which the boy's father sometimes reads aloud, declaiming with broad gestures "Excelsior" or "The Curfew Must Not Ring Tonight"; here the boy is a scholar. For he believes in the magical notion that knowledge is power.

ONE CHRISTMAS

the boy carves three pine Nativity figures. Jesus is easy, the swaddling cloths a lump needing only a slash here and there for wrinkles. The demure ridge of

Mary's bust gives the boy some trouble, but it is Joseph's beard which makes him cut himself. Until he paints it, the white wooden face bears the dried blood like a birthmark.

A RERUN

is the best kind of show to watch on television. With stock formats, you know even the first time around how things will generally turn out. Just as you know generally that your life will end in death. But a rerun gives you godly presience of particulars.

I am watching a western for the third time. It's B- as Rory Calhoun (the bad man in films of B+ pretensions) is the hero, and the bad man is a nameless (perhaps, his dreams disappointed, alcoholic, divorced) bit-player achieving a brief, dubious, supporting stardom.

The bad man's problem is anyone's: He is free to turn himself in (giving up his gun and nature), or be on the noon stage, or die. The respites given him by the upbeat commercials are illusory. The film he lives in blurs the individual still frames into believeable motion, leaving him no room to stop, or turn, start over, as he careers in the eye of light, a paradigm of habit, making the same mistaken choices, wrongly believing again he will yet win out — right into the recalled moment of silence when as if to scratch his arm his fingers creep to the pearl grip of a sleeve-holstered derringer. A .44 slug shatters his heart and possibility.

"He didn't know when to quit," the marshall says.

The credits are given, a gloss to the fable.

Two years ago I wrote and published a poem on this subject. Which makes the present section an example of a recurrent theme, and a rerun.

INVISIBLE INK

is lemon juice and the boy writes secret messages to his parents, leaving them about in the apartment for their discovery. His mother mistakes them for waste paper and throws most away. The boy takes one to his father but it catches fire over the candle.

He watches the slow graceful browning curl of the paper, his message becoming visible as a thin stream of grey rising and disappearing into the air.

"Smoke signals," his father jokes.

A JACK OF ALL TRADES

is what people call the boy's father. The mother is enfuriated by his acting as if it were a compliment.

"Well, isn't it true? My name is Jack, and just what can't I do if I set my mind to it? You tell me. Okay, I'll tell you. Nothing, that's what."

A small-time entrepreneur who, as if hurrying to some better place, runs through a used-furniture store, corner grocery, hole-in-the-wall diner, hot-dog stand, and home mail order business selling keyrings and lockets, he is also at times a newspaper reporter, appliance salesman, used car salesman, failed inventor, and publisher of "Illusions", a small collection of his own relentlessly rhymed verse — which he fails to convince local bookstores to carry and so gives out to relatives and, finally, passes out on streetcorners where even though the copies are free many refuse to accept them.

TECHNIQUES OF WOOD-CARVING

are important. Otherwise you can ruin whatever it is you are trying to make; your project, let's say.

Always go with the grain.

Always move the knife blade away from you. There is no need to cause yourself unnecessary pain through ignorance, when there is ample pain necessitated by knowledge.

Myself, I wear two scars on the tip of my left thumb. Months apart, they were both caused by my excitement blotting out remembrance of the rules. Though I didn't see it in time then, from this distance I can picture the blade sliding toward me, behind it a thin curling strip of white wood like a spring coiled to push the steel into my thumb.

The scars lie parallel, a half an inch apart, like parentheses enclosing that period of my life when I first began fashioning images of how I saw the world.

THE THING

is the boy's favorite movie. How neighborhood audiences shriek seeing that hair suit freed of its paralyzing ice block by the heat of human discovery!

Of course the Thing's discoverers, repelled by its lack

of recognizable form, shriek too. And destroy it for the good of civilization.

PLAYING GAMES (ALONE)

is the way the boy spends the entire summer when he is eleven and his father goes to the hospital and his mother takes a job dishing out food in a cafeteria.

The boy's back "yard" is the roof of a furniture warehouse which connects to the shops beneath the apartments and runs back to face the alley. The boy bounces a rubber ball off the kitchen door, an imagined announcer yelling, "It's a hit!", and then as he scoops up the return, "Cody's got it!", calling it a marvellous save.

When he misses, the ball rolls down the slight decline to land in the gutter lipping the roof. The boy lies flat on his belly to reach out into the rusty trough. Two years later, going onto the roof at all will dizzy him and he will keep far back from the edge.

On the couch those summer mornings, forcing down the growing awareness of more exciting play, he makes a game of throwing one of the small couch pillows at the ceiling. At first he merely tosses it up and tries to catch it, but this soon bores him. He experiments and discovers it is difficult to throw the pillow so it barely touches the ceiling. Thrown too easy it falls short; too hard it bounces back nearly impossible to catch.

He tosses for himself first, softly, the pillow's rise ending just short of the ceiling. "Cody misses!", a part of him announces in his head. Then a third part, a competitor given the neighbor's name, Fowler, throws — "Too hard!" The pillow shoots back to one side and he misses it. "Zero-zero. Round two."

Cody beats Fowler with craft. He perfects his throw so that the pillow goes up, end over end, and — just at that moment gravity's mounting weight initiates the inevitable fall — kisses the ceiling, the boy's hands waiting below like a fireman's net.

FICTION,

just as games are fictive, is a game. What do you risk by reading it? Irretrievable time? Artificially stimulated emotions? In rare moments meeting yourself? Still, characters will not physically break from the page to throttle you.

They have been known to do this to the writer. Dickens was held captive and eventually killed by his escaped criminals: Nick Adams grew up embittered to shotgun old man Hemingway.

It is in the nature of the created to turn against the creator. Like children, they begin home-life with kicks in mother's belly, and end it — declaring independence in Hyde-like adolescence — with kicks in father's teeth.

TOUCHING

is a natural act. But dangerous. Reaching out is always a risk. Somebody might break your fingers shaking your hand. With a kiss give you a disease.

"Don't touch me!" the boy hears his mother say

sharply in the dark. And later: "You heard me."

PLAYING GAMES (TOGETHER)

is more fun than alone. Again out of work, the boy's father spends days making up a game he calls "Lucky". He roughs it out with the boy's crayons on a sheet of cardboard, reciting as he does the story of the rich and respected Parker Brothers and how they had come up with Monopoly when they were down and out during the Depression.

He and the boy take turns rolling the dice and moving thimbles along a maze of small squares trying to be the first to reach a large red square in the center of the board. The boy enjoys the game, but his father is unable to work out the details and — just as the boy's mother predicts — it comes to nothing. The father goes back out looking for jobs; another game, he says.

Although the boy doesn't realize it (shaking the dice in his hand under his father's eye), he loves games for the same reason we all do. They allow us to play at the real, yet (as the real ultimately does not) allow us to escape intact. No matter how recklessly you play Monopoly, you risk only paper. The most complex chess problems seems a kindergarten dot-to-dot compared to the factors involved in making any real life decision — whether or not to believe what someone swears is true, knowing that affirmation means roping yourself to the other on a high, ice-patched ledge; whether or not to look back over your shoulder at the shadow dogging your tracks.

OLD MAXIMS

are often wrong. For instance, "seeing is believing". Some things you see but can't believe, like a man dropping out of the sky. Rather, what you believe is what you see. What was it but deep belief made Saint Teresa experience an orgasm as Divine Visitation? And who are we to call her wrong?

The night the boy awakes on the living room couch that is his bed, he hushes his breathing to hear a snuffling in the hallway. Has it come in the back door? There is a scratching at the door to his parents' bedroom. A werewolf? Why doesn't his father wake up and fight it?

The boy sees a shadow coming on all fours into the living room. As in a dream, he cannot make a sound. The werewolf reaches him. A hand gropes for his face. Then the whiskey smell and a furry voice; "There y'are. Ah, who's my boy, huh?"

THE NEW DODGE

is what prompts his father to bring the boy and his mother to the front room window, making them keep their eyes shut. He snaps his fingers — "Open sez me!" — and the boy is awe-struck. A glittering black 1953 Dodge sedan!

"Is it ours? Is it ours?"

His father tells him it is.

"To keep?"

"Sure!"

The boy's mother leaves the living room, her heels clacking against the linoleum.

"Can we go for a ride? Anywhere? Please!"

Later — like the cigarette his father can hold, wave his hand and, when the boy uncurls the stained fingers, make disappear — the car is gone. The vacant spot at the curb seems doubly so to the boy, as if the air there held an emptiness shaped like a Dodge sedan.

He understands, even at twelve, that he has learned something about how real things aren't.

THE SPIT AND IMAGE

the boy hears his mother say again. He has forgotten to do his homework. "The spit and image!" His mouth opens to speak, but he hangs between pride and shame, and is silent.

FALLING

over the brink of his childhood into his teens, the boy catches onto his father's trick. At the crucial pause he grabs at the shirt pocket and uncovers the cigarette.

"Hey", his father complains, "what do you want to go and spoil it for?"

THE SECOND CAR

is a year old — "As good as new, inside and out!" — red '53 Chevvie hardtop. It is to last three months before, as the boy expects, it disappears.

"What do you mean you don't want to go? Are you kidding? C'mon, I'll let you steer."

The boy goes to the kitchen with his mother. The flat bang of the slammed door leaves the apartment seeming too quiet; like just before the Indians attack in westerns, he thinks.

He has a problem with division and his mother sits beside him over the math book open on the table. She leans forward to point out his error, her breast brushing his forearm.

3-D

was a true art form. It was forceful and immediate. (The boy jerks back his head expecting to be hit in the face by a juggler's ball in "The House of Wax".) It sprang from that universal impulse which gives rise to the exaggerated perspectives — the gnarled hands seeming to thrust beyond the illustration's frame — of the comic books the boy is reading in the living room armchair. It is the impulse at the root of this story I am struggling with in my study (my coffee gone cold, my single pipe oversmoked until it burns my tongue). To reach out and touch, cross time lines, break boundaries—

FLIGHT

is what the boy believes his father tries from the roof of the apartment house.

I know, I know. At fourteen, he ought to know better. He realizes this too, But the boy is, and as a man will remain, possessed by a need for belief.

We make our choices and live by them. To live by them.

AND MY CHEATING

is the result of the undertaking. Honest Abe is the Big Lie.

Telling you a story peopled by ghosts, I conjure you to feel as real what is imaginary. Adjectives form a chant, verbs order nouns to rise and walk.

Believe me.

YOU

are the reader and, though you've not suspected it, I know you. Remember the night I saw you at the newsstand? You were wearing brown shoes and a grey coat and bought a comic book called "The Phantom Stranger". I admired your refusal to apologize to the clerk.

Another time, on the subway, I spotted you reading a correspondence school flier.

(Ads and catalogs coax us to believe in possibility. Other places, other jobs, other possessions would transform us: We would become the selves we know we really are, not these mock-ups with which we are forced to make do.

The flier offered a home study course in accounting. Did you ever send for it? If so, what do you account for now?

AT THE END

of the magazines the boy reads during his high-school years are always the Charles Atlas cartoons showing some poor misfit getting sand kicked in his face. The boy never gets up the nerve to send for the 32 page illustrated booklet, "How Dynamic Tension Makes you a NEW MAN". He becomes one anyway, as all boys do. But with the same old flaws. And a new one. Now he writes stories to redeem a lost past, and they fail.

Gaming

There was no front way to Lucy Wenner's. The long outside flight of grey wooden stairs led to the kitchen door. Once the back door, it was now the only one, for the apartment was half its former self. The living room and bedroom had been blocked off years before Lucy moved in (that, eight years past, right after her husband, Earl, died in the fire of his jack-knifed semi) to form an office above the downstairs barber shop.

A lawyer just out of school held the office now. He was so young, Price thought, he still talked about justice instead of law.

Ed Price, wearing clean green twill workpants and a pressed white shirt, tieless and open-collared, waited before the kitchen door. Behind him, the stairs creaked under the monstrous weight of Marty Gratz.

Violet shadows of early evening relieved the drabness of the grey porch and wall. A high small kitchen window was pale yellow with light; the four square panes like pats of margarine.

Marty succeeded in mounting the stairs. He stood sucking wind, his face beaded in sweat like a basted turkey.

"What if she gets mad? She could call the cops."

Price waved the boy into silence and rapped his knuckles against the door. It opened to linoleum and a hanging bare bulb. A boy of six hung on the knob.

"Hello Lucky," Price said.

"Who is it?" a woman's voice asked.

The boy turned. "Mister Price."

"Whiteshirt?" Lucy came into the light. She had tinted her hair reddish in the months since Price had last caught sight of her downtown. To cover grey? he wondered. His own hair showed salt and pepper at the temples now. His face had creased with the strain of forty-eight years of managing day to day life.

By now she had to be at least forty.

But she was still a woman a man noticed, even in the cotton house dress she wore. Her body's fullness promised ease.

Though Price knew better.

"What brings you here?"

"See how you are."

"Sure."

"Lucky," Price said to the boy, "you're shooting up like a weed."

"Who's your friend?" Lucy asked.

"Marty. He works with me."

Marty leaned to one side to look past Price's shoulder. "Hi," he said.

"Hi."

"Pleased to meet you."

"You want to come in?" Lucy said to Price.

"If you're not busy."

"I'm home from work, why should I be busy?"

"You want me to go?"

"I didn't say that." Lucy took a step back and motioned them in. Marty sidled to the refrigerator and leaned his back against it, studying the floor. Price stood in the center of the room.

Two girls in their pre-teens sat at the kitchen table with the boy. They had been playing Monopoly.

"Who's winning?" Price asked.

"Mom," one of the girls said.

"Figures. You got a head for business, Lucy."

"Look who's talking." She had tugged straight the faded green dress and tightened its belt. She brushed her hair back with one hand.

"She's got Boardwalk and Park Place," the other girl said. "Houses on them too."

"Can we play?" the boy whined. "It's my turn!"

"In a bit, Eddie," Lucy said; then to Price, "You want to watch us play or what?"

"I'd like to talk to you."

"Go ahead."

Price moved past her, going into the adjoining room. "Wait just a minute!" she was saying.

The room was a combined living room and bedroom. It had two windows at one side and Price went to one and looked down on an alley. He heard Lucy telling the children to go ahead and play. Then she came into the room and closed the door.

"What's the big idea?"

He didn't look away from the window. He thought he could feel the heat of her body warm the air around him. "How you been doing?"

"What's it to you?"

"You make enough at the plant to get along?"

"I do just fine."

"Got plenty of friends there no doubt."

"What if I do?"

He turned and looked down at her. "Don't get me wrong. What you do is your business."

"I know that."

"I'm not asking for myself."

"Asking what?"

"If you're still in business."

"You sonuvabitch!"

"Take it easy," Price said. "It's nothing to me one way or the other."

"Sure."

"It isn't. I just wanted to know."

"Who for?"

Price jerked his head at the door. Lucy's eyebrows jumped. "You got to be kidding."

"He'll end up in a nuthouse unless some woman treats him right."

"You're crazy, Whiteshirt. You know what you're asking?"

"Look, we're adults, right?"

"I can only speak for myself."

"Let's not fight about it. I hear him every day, whining. No woman will look at him twice. He's a sick kid. He needs help."

"Take him to a doctor."

"Have a heart."

"You can say that to me? To me?"

"Keep your voice down, will you?"

"Here we go again. Keep your voice down, Lucy. Act like nothing's wrong, Lucy. Take it easy, Lucy."

Price stepped away from the window. "I thought I'd be doing you a favor."

"Sure."

"You need the money don't you?"

Lucy's open hand smacked against his cheek, knocking loose two strands of Price's oiled black forelock. He didn't move.

"Big-hearted, aren't you? You low bastard!"

"Canning season's almost over, isn't it? You got another job lined up?"

"I get along without any help from you. Believe me, I don't need it. I don't need you one bit. Not for anything."

Price sighed. He smoothed his hair back in place, touched his cheek. "I just thought maybe the charity wasn't enough."

"Don't try to rub my nose in it, Whiteshirt, cause it won't work. Not anymore."

"What do you mean?"

"It's A.D.C. I'm a citizen, I got rights. I get nothing but what I'm entitled to. Less, if you ask me. If Earl's pension fund had been better . . ."

"We'd never have gotten together."

Lucy stepped forward, her shoulders sagging a bit. "You make me be so hard with you. You never give me a chance to be anything else. Your whore! All you had to do, Whiteshirt, was to say yes."

Price turned to walk slowly about the room. Beyond the couch and easy chair facing the T.V., there were bunkbeds and a large brown pasteboard wardrobe. A curtained alcove held, he knew, Lucy's bed. "I guess I'll go."

"I'm old enough to be his mother," Lucy said.

"And I could be his father. So what?"

"I'm getting too old."

"Quit feeling sorry for yourself."

"If I don't, who will? You?"

"Look, you're not hurting me saying no. Go take a look at him. The poor slob is ready to cut his throat or hang himself."

"Let him." Her upper lip curled. "Listen, I'm onto you. You don't lord it over me anymore, hear?"

"What do you think I'm trying to pull? I'm trying to help out is all."

"You? You never cared about anybody . . . Where you going?"

"I didn't come here for a sermon."

"Wait a minute."

"What for?"

"Maybe I'll do it."

"Make up your mind, will you?"

"Not for the money though. Or for him. For you."

"What are you talking about? It's him wants it, not me."

"For you as a favor. You ask me nice. Say please."

"For Chrissakes."

"I'm not kidding, Whiteshirt. Ask me, please, or get out."

"I just don't understand you."

"You never did. Well?"

"All right. Please. There, you satisfied."

"Tell him to come in."

Price opened the door and called Marty. The fat boy hurried across the kitchen. "Look," he whispered, "if she don't . . ."

"It's all right. Come on."

"I could hear you, she was arguing. I don't wanna cause any trouble."

"It's all set." Price look at the children at the table. "Who's winning?"

"Nobody yet," one of the girls said.

"Where's Mom?" the boy asked.

"She'll be right out. Got to talk about something." He hissed to Marty, "You want it or not? Come on. She'll treat you right."

"I don't know. You were arguing." Price took Marty's arm and pulled him into the room. "I wanna go," Marty whispered.

Lucy had gone to the alcove, now she returned. She was still wearing her dress, but Price noticed her shoes were gone. He guessed that she had taken off her panties.

"Go on." He pushed Marty toward her.

The fat boy stood stranded for a moment, then Lucy came to him and took his hands in hers. "Marty," she said. "Aren't you a big young man. I'll bet you're strong as an ox."

Price stood, intrigued by her crisp movements, the certainty in her voice. She seemed alert, self-possessed, a professional.

This was the woman he needed to remember. This was how she was when he first met her, before her softening into slumped shoulders, eyes puffed from crying, a belly beginning to swell.

"Watch the door for us, will you?" Lucy asked.

Price moved to go into the kitchen.

"No, Whiteshirt, here. The girls will think something's funny if you leave the two of us in here alone."

"He's not gonna stay?" Marty's voice rose to a near-squeak.

"He has to," Lucy said. "My girls."

"I don't want him staying."

"He won't look. Will you, Whiteshirt."

"No," Price said.

"See? Now come on, come over here." Lucy led Marty to the alcove. He waited for her to arrange the bed, but instead she asked him to lie down on the floor. He looked, as if for rescue, back at the door. Price glanced away.

"No offense, honey," Lucy was saying, "but the bed, well, it's small, don't you see? If we break it, where would I sleep? You don't want me to have to sleep on the floor, do you?" She maintained a soothing banter as she managed, like a mahout training a young elephant, to get the boy down on his back. "And you're just too big a man to be on top. You see what I mean, don't you? I'm sure you don't want to hurt me now, do you? And I won't hurt you. Here, it's all right. Let me get your belt."

Marty lay with the top of his head toward Price. His trousers opened, Lucy knelt beside him in the interior dusk, her hand working. Then she slid her dress up her thighs and rose to settle over the boy's hardness, a hen on an egg. She began rocking slowly back and forth. "There," she said, her eyes on Price. "How's that? Nice, huh?"

Marty grunted. His arms were outspread, hands flat on the floor as if hanging onto the spinning world. He seemed to Price to be a beached, water-bloated body; Lucy, a lifeguard working to stir the still flesh back into action.

Price imagined beneath the airy fan of Lucy's skirt the fleshed thighs pressed sweating spread about the fat boy's hips. He could hear her hole working, like a suction cup applied by a nurse to draw out poison. She fascinated him. Skilled in her craft, she employed her tool with an efficiency beyond shame.

Price felt himself warm and grow. He tugged at the stiff fly of his trousers and was caught off-guard by Lucy's laugh.

The bitch, he thought.

He straightened and leaned back against the door, folding his arms across his chest.

Behind him he heard a girl's voice claim eight hundred dollars rent — "it has four houses" — and the boy begging her to accept the Utilities in trade so he could stay in the game.

Price, unblinking, met Lucy's look. He smiled to show his utter lack of discomfort.

"Just fine," Lucy said. She leaned back, her hands braced on her thighs, arching her back. "You do just fine, honey. Just fine."

She leaned forward then to pull Marty's hands from the floor. She planted them against her covered breasts where they stuck like barnacles. Her hands on Marty's shoulders, she began pumping up and down the bell-curved mass of her hips and rump and belly, moving deep, relentlessly. Marty whimpered. Lucy bared her teeth in a grin.

Price felt a sudden surprising rush of anger at the boy enjoying a woman he had no right to.

He checked his anger. Right had nothing to do with it. You got what you paid for.

He knew her game. He swore she would not make

him jealous. Any man misses what's gone, he thought, it's the fool tries to go back.

In you want out; out you want in.

Price looked down at the two figures joined on the floor. He pressed back reawakening feelings as if suffocating a bed-partner with a pillow, instead etching in his mind the remembered wrinkles about her eyes, the sag of flesh beneath her chin.

Some prize, he thought. Wearing out with use. No wonder she wants somebody to take care of her.

How her girls would talk about her once they learned the truth! And the boy, a whore for a mother! What could any father say to change that?

A cheap whore. He felt comforted by the simplicity of the words. A cheap whore. A cheap whore.

They sat at a table to the rear of the Cozy Corner, Price taking the chair against the wall. He ordered a beer for each of them and a shot for himself. He held up the shotglass between thumb and forefinger, dipping his head to look through the clear amber at the round face opposite him. "Here's to you, a man of the world." He downed the shot.

Marty managed a clownish smile.

Price slowly poured half the bottle of beer into his glass. An even quarter-inch head rose above the rim and held there, a contained quavering. "You hear about the whores getting mad at the bartender for putting salt in their Schlitz?"

"Uh-uh." Marty ran two fingers around and around the circled lip of his glass.

"It's a joke, stupid."

"Oh."

"Drink your beer. You earned it."

"You pay her?"

"I left it on the dresser."

"She said not to."

"She was kidding."

"How do you know?"

"I know."

"Why would she say it if she didn't mean it?"

"Women. Who knows?"

Marty's body swayed to one side as if he meant to pass gas. He dug in a back pocket. "I'll pay you back."

"Forget it."

"I wanna." He opened a worn black billfold.

"You can buy the drinks."

"It was more."

"Forget it, I said. Maybe now you'll keep your mind on your work, not have me picking up your end all the time."

"What d'you mean? I work."

"Who do you think you're kidding? You been mooning around like a sick cow. I load more packages in an hour than you do in a day."

"Well, I was . . ."

"You want to pay me back, just keep your mind on your work."

"I try to."

"Then do it. You got your piece now. Relax."

Marty's eyes drooped in a hurt look. He drank from his glass, then began toying with it again. "I wish I was married."

"To her?"

Marty shrugged. "She's nice."

"On two bucks an hour? What'd you have her do, take in boarders? Like that landlady got caught spreading roomers?"

"Hey, c'mon!"

"Some husband you'd make! Save your money for Friday nights, you're better off."

"I don't know."

"I know, that's why I'm telling you."

Price finished his beer and ordered another with a shot. Each night he had two beers, two shots, never anymore, even when someone else was buying. He saw too many of the old boys bellied up to the bar, day and night, slaves.

He recalled a coal miner who had sat beside him once. The man's face and hands were a dead dry black. Price had watched him take a long drink of his beer, then wipe his lips to leave an ash-grey blur about his mouth.

All the boys at the bar were burnt-out, Price thought. Old houses whose furnaces got too hot.

Stoke it, stoke it, that heat feels oh so good!

The miner had sat and stared at his big-knuckled

blackened hands as if they were chunks of rubbish raked from the ashes.

Price glanced at Marty. What could he know. A hog, he wanted it all. He'd be another one belly-aching about bills, the wife's female troubles, the girl with measles, how there was nothing could straighten out that boy, stealing hubcaps now, how when he himself was young he'd never once thought . . .

None of them did. Their heads were to hold their hats.

In the morning Price would come down from his room at seven, have one egg, over, white toast, black coffee and a glass of grapefruit juice. At seven-thirty he would punch in. On the dock — he rapped his knuckles lightly against the wooden table top, again recognizing his luck to be in parcels rather than backbreaking freight — he would load, stopping twice for coffee, once for lunch, until four. He had the evenings to himself.

"Hey, Whiteshirt!"

A waitress was pointing at him. Price started up, then sat, seeing the small figure threading the tables to him.

The boy stopped beside Price's chair. He looked down at his holey black sneakers.

"Hey," Marty whispered. "Isn't this her kid?"

" 'Course he's her kid. Who'd you think he was?"

The boy looked too thin to Price. What was he doing out this late anyway? Didn't she know any better?

The boy mumbled something.

"What?"

As if afraid to speak again, the boy unclenched a fist and dropped two crumpled ten dollar bills onto the table.

"What do you think you're doing?" The boy flinched, and Price softened his voice. "Your mom tell you to do this?"

The boy nodded.

"What'd I tell you," Marty said. "Didn't I tell you she didn't want it?"

"Shuttup."

"But I was right, wasn't I?"

"Shuttup before I toss your fat ass outta here." Price lay a hand on the boy's boney shoulder. "I don't want this. This belongs to your mom."

"She said."

Why the boy? The girls were older, one of them should have come. Did she hate him that much? How could she say she loved him for what he was and hate him for what he was?

"She said you can't come see us anymore."

"I knew she was mad," Marty started, but Price waved him into silence. He picked up the two bills and flattened them against the table with the palm of a hand, slowly smoothing them back and forth. The boy moved to go. "Hold it," Price said. He lay one bill atop the other, folded the two in halves, quarters, eighths. He stuck the small green wad into the boy's shirt pocket and pushed the boy's hand away.

"Listen son, this is going to be our secret. Just ours.

I was a good friend of your daddy's. He wanted me to help look after you. So that money's yours. You keep it. Hide it someplace. You don't have to tell your mom, she won't ever know. It's yours. You need it sometime, then you'll have it. You understand what I'm telling you?"

The boy nodded.

"And something else. This is way too late for you to be out. You ought to be in bed. You have to get your sleep and eat right, you want to grow up strong. You listening to me?"

"She said she liked it," the boy said.

"What?"

"She said you knew." The boy turned to Marty. "And to tell you thanks."

Marty grinned widely.

"Well, goddamn!" Price said. He patted the boy's shoulder. "You get on home and get to bed. Go on."

When the boy had gone, Price sipped his beer in silence. Twice Marty cleared his throat as if to speak. Finally he asked, "How come you gave him the money? Lucy said . . ."

"Lucy? Shit!"

"Well she said she didn't want it, didn't she? Why'd you give it to him? Maybe she just wanted to have some fun."

"It's my weakness," Price said. "Yours is being stupid, mine's being too big-hearted." He emptied his glass and leaned back in the chair. "I am a generous man."